The Spice of Love

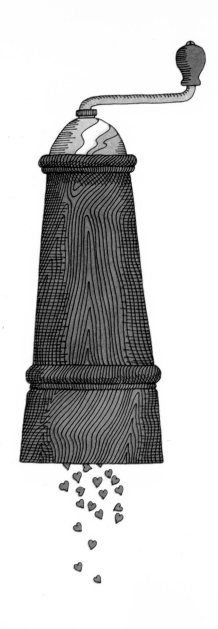

The Spice of Love

Wisdom and Wit About Love
Through the Ages

Selected by Robert Myers
Accented With Satiric Color
Illustrations by John Trotta

HALLMARK EDITIONS

Wisdom and Wit About Love
Through the Ages

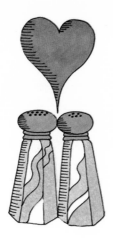

To live is like to love—all reason is against it, and all healthy instinct is for it.

Samuel Butler

Men always want to be a woman's first love, women like to be a man's last romance.

Oscar Wilde

In love, there is always one who kisses and one who offers the cheek. *French Proverb*

No woman ever hates a man for being in love with her; but many a woman hates a man for being a friend to her. *Alexander Pope*

Marriage has many pains, but celibacy has no pleasures. *Samuel Johnson*

Next to being married, a girl likes to be crossed in love a little now and then. *Jane Austen*

Tell a woman she is beautiful, and the devil will repeat it to her ten times.
Italian Proverb

It is easier to be a lover than a husband, for the same reason that it is more difficult to show a ready wit all day long than to say a good thing occasionally. *Honore de Balzac*

If they only married when they fell in love, most people would die unwed.
R. L. Stevenson

Good is when I steal other people's wives and cattle; bad is when they steal mine.
Hottentot Proverb

Love is the history of a woman's life; it is an episode in man's. *Mme. de Stael*

Variety's the very spice of life,
That gives it all its flavor. *William Cowper*

When Eve saw her reflection in a pool, she sought Adam and accused him of infidelity.
Ambrose Bierce

Brigands demand your money or your life; women require both. *Samuel Butler*

Love is not altogether a delirium, yet it has many points in common therewith.
Thomas Carlyle

The loves of some people are but the result of good suppers. *Sebastien Chamfort*

There can be only one end to marriage without love, and that is love without marriage.
John Collins

Love and scandal are the best sweeteners of tea. *Henry Fielding*

When a woman is speaking to you, listen to what she says with her eyes. *Victor Hugo*

If men knew all that women think, they'd be twenty times more daring. *Alphonse Karr*

Chaste is she whom no one has asked. *Ovid*

Marriage resembles a pair of shears, so joined that they can not be separated; often moving in opposite directions, yet always punishing anyone who comes between them.

Sydney Smith

Women in love pardon great indiscretions more easily than little infidelities.

La Rochefoucauld

There's nothing half so sweet in life as love's young dream. *Thomas Moore*

Remember, it's as easy to marry a rich woman as a poor woman. *Thackeray*

To write a love letter we must begin without knowing what we intend to say, and end without knowing what we have written.

Jean Jacques Rousseau

By all means marry; if you get a good wife, you'll become happy; if you get a bad one, you'll become a philosopher. *Socrates*

Lord, I wonder what fool it was that first invented kissing. *Jonathan Swift*

In order to avoid being called a flirt, she always yielded easily. *Talleyrand*

In love, one always begins by deceiving oneself, and one always ends by deceiving others; that is what the world calls a romance.
Oscar Wilde

Everything is sweetened by risk.
Alexander Smith

The girl who can't dance says the band can't play. *Yiddish Proverb*

It is good to be without vice, but it is not good to be without temptations. *Walter Bagehot*

A dog is the only thing on this earth that loves you more than he loves himself.
Josh Billings

Man is the only animal that blushes
—or needs to. *Mark Twain*

If God considered woman a helpmeet for man, he must have had a very poor opinion of man.
Samuel Butler

I never knew but one woman who would not take gold—and she took diamonds.
Horace Walpole

Woman's vanity demands that a man be more than a happy husband. *Nietzsche*

I should like to know what is the proper function of women, if it is not to make reasons for husbands to stay at home, and still stronger reasons for bachelors to go out. *George Eliot*

If women were by nature what they make themselves by artifice, if their faces suddenly became as bright or as leaden as they make them with paint and powder, they would be inconsolable. *Jean de La Bruyere*

We are ashamed to admit that we are jealous, but proud that we were and that we can be. *La Rochefoucauld*

What is irritating about love is that it is a crime that requires an accomplice. *Charles Baudelaire*

Dost thou think, because thou art virtuous, there shall be no more cakes and ale? *Shakespeare*

The wise want love; and those who love want wisdom. *Shelley*

Love's the noblest frailty of the mind. *John Dryden*

God created woman. And boredom did indeed cease from that moment — but many other things ceased as well! Woman was God's *second* mistake. *Nietzsche*

11

Nothing reopens the springs of love so fully as absence, and no absence so thoroughly as that which must needs be endless.

Anthony Trollope

O love, O lover, loose or hold me fast,
I had thee first, whoever have thee last.

Swinburne

Who marrieth for love without money hath good nights and sorry days. *John Ray*

Every woman should marry—and no man.

Benjamin Disraeli

Most females will forgive a liberty, rather than a slight, and if any woman were to hang a man for stealing her picture, although it were set in gold, it would be a new case in law; but if he carried off the setting, and left the portrait, I would not answer for his safety.   *C. C. Colton*

Whoever thinks of going to bed before twelve o'clock is a scoundrel.   *Samuel Johnson*

The resistance of a woman is not always a proof of her virtue but more frequently of her experience.   *Ninon de Lenclos*

It goes far toward reconciling me to being a woman when I reflect that I am thus in no danger of marrying one.
   Mary Wortley Montagu

13

Woman will be the last thing civilized by man.
George Meredith

To be constant in love to one is good; to be constant to many is great.   *J. J. Roche*

Marriage is the only adventure open to the cowardly.   *Voltaire*

A man can be happy with any woman as long as he does not love her.   *Oscar Wilde*

Woman inspires us to great things, and prevents us from achieving them.
Alexandre Dumas

I have met with women whom I really think would like to be married to a poem, and to be given away by a novel.   *John Keats*

The impassioned man hasn't time to be witty.
Stendhal

A good husband makes a good wife.
Robert Burton

All women are good — good for nothing, or good for something.   *Cervantes*

14

A man who is absolutely in love does not know whether he is more or less in love than others, for anyone who knows this is, just on that account, not absolutely in love.

Soren Kierkegaard

It is a mistake to speak of a bad choice in love, since, as soon as a choice exists, it can only be bad.   *Marcel Proust*

If you are afraid of loneliness, don't marry.

Anton Chekhov

I wish Adam had died with all his ribs in his body.   *Dion Boucicault*

She laughs at everything you say. Why? Because she has fine teeth.

Benjamin Franklin

Man has his will, but woman has her way.

Oliver Wendell Holmes

Who loves not women, wine and song remains a fool his whole life long.   *Martin Luther*

To a quick question, give a slow answer.

Italian Proverb

Here's to woman! Would that we could fall into her arms without falling into her hands.

Ambrose Bierce

Women give themselves to God when the Devil wants nothing more to do with them.

Sophie Arnould

So heavy is the chain of wedlock that it needs two to carry it, and sometimes three.

Alexandre Dumas

Women are such expensive things.

George Meredith

As soon as Eve ate the apple of wisdom, she reached for the fig leaf; when a woman begins to think, her first thought is of a new dress.

Heinrich Heine

A wife is to thank God her husband has faults; a husband without faults is a dangerous observer. *Marquis of Halifax*

The only comfort of my life
Is that I never yet had wife.
Robert Herrick

Hatred is by far the longest pleasure;
Men love in haste, but they detest at leisure.
Lord Byron

Love is said to be blind, but I know lots of fellows in love who can see twice as much in their sweethearts as I can. *Josh Billings*

When the blind lead the blind, they both fall into—matrimony. *George Farquhar*

One can find women who have never had one love affair, but it is rare indeed to find any who have had only one. *La Rochefoucauld*

There is but one hour a day between a good housewife and a bad one. *English Proverb*

Love does not dominate; it cultivates.
Goethe

Tact is the intelligence of the heart.
Anonymous

The fundamental fault of the female character is that it has no sense of justice.
Arthur Schopenhauer

Can you recall a woman who ever showed you with pride her library?
Benjamin De Casseres

A modest woman, dressed out in all her finery, is the most tremendous object of the whole creation. *Oliver Goldsmith*

The silliest woman can manage a clever man, but it needs a very clever woman to manage a fool. *Rudyard Kipling*

A man too good for the world is no good for his wife. *Yiddish Proverb*

Love, and do what you will.

Saint Augustine

Man's love is of man's life a thing apart, 'Tis woman's whole existence. *Lord Byron*

Sir, it is so far from being natural for a man and a woman to live in a state of marriage, that we find all the motives that they have for remaining in that connection, and the restraints which civilized society imposes to prevent separation, are hardly sufficient to keep them together. *Samuel Johnson*

A wise woman never yields by appointment.

Stendhal

Love is ever the beginning of Knowledge, as fire is of light. *Thomas Carlyle*

The supreme happiness of life is the conviction that we are loved. *Victor Hugo*

God is Love, I dare say. But what a mischievous devil Love is. *Samuel Butler*

Better to sit up all night, than to go to bed with a dragon. *Jeremy Taylor*

It is a mistake for a taciturn, serious-minded woman to marry a jovial man, but not for a serious-minded man to marry a lighthearted woman. *Goethe*

Lovely female shapes are terrible complicators of the difficulties and dangers of this earthly life, especially for their owner.

George Du Maurier

Perfect Love casts out Prudery together with Fear. *Richard Garnett*

It is a great consolation to reflect that, among all the bewildering changes to which the world is subject, the character of woman cannot be altered. *Coventry Patmore*

Grief can take care of itself, but to get the full value of a joy you must have somebody to divide it with. *Mark Twain*

Stolen sweets are always sweeter;
Stolen kisses much completer;
Stolen looks are nice in chapels;
Stolen, stolen be your apples. *Leigh Hunt*

Strange to say what delight we married people have to see these poor fools decoyed into our condition. *Samuel Pepys*

It is as absurd to say that a man can't love one woman all the time as it is to say that a violinist needs several violins to play the same piece of music. *Honore de Balzac*

Who can find a virtuous woman? for her price
is far above rubies.   *Old Testament*

Though marriage makes man and wife one
flesh, it leaves them still two fools.
                        William Congreve

Love lessens woman's delicacy and increases
man's.   *Jean Paul Richter*

The only difference between a caprice and a
lifelong passion is that the caprice lasts a little
longer.   *Oscar Wilde*

Whoever loves, if he do not propose
The right true end of love, he's one that goes
To sea for nothing but to make him sick.
                        John Donne

Love seeketh not itself to please,
Nor for itself hath any care,
But for another gives its ease,
And builds a Heaven in Hell's despair.
                        William Blake

Let us embrace, and from this very
moment vow an eternal misery together.
                        Thomas Otway

The surest way to hit a woman's heart is to take aim kneeling.   *D. W. Jerrold*

Love is a species of melancholy.
                                        Robert Burton

As to marriage or celibacy, let a man take which course he will, he will be sure to repent.
                                        Socrates

Happiness is the perpetual possession of being well deceived.   *Jonathan Swift*

Men were born to lie, and women to believe them.   *John Gay*

There swims no goose so gray, but soon or late,
She finds some honest gander for her mate.
                                        Alexander Pope

Self-love is a cup without any bottom; you might pour all the great lakes into it, and never fill it up.   *Oliver Wendell Holmes*

A man would create another man if one did not already exist, but a woman might live an eternity without even thinking of reproducing her own sex.   *Goethe*

Courtship consists in a number of quiet attentions, not so pointed as to alarm, nor so vague as not to be understood.   *Laurence Sterne*

Life is a tragedy for those who feel, and a comedy for those who think.
                                        Jean de La Bruyere

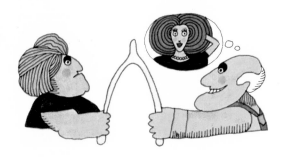

If a man could have half his wishes, he would double his troubles.   *Benjamin Franklin*

What cannot be cured must be endured.
                                        Rabelais

Don't marry for money; you can borrow it cheaper.   *Scotch Proverb*

A woman seldom asks advice before she has bought her wedding clothes.   *Addison*

It is better to dwell in a corner of the house-top, than with a brawling woman in a wide house. *Old Testament*

For love, all love of other sights controls,
And makes one little room, an everywhere.
John Donne

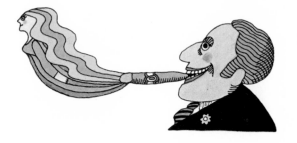

A woman is only a woman, but a good cigar is a smoke. *Rudyard Kipling*

Habit is everything—even in love.
Marquis de Vauvenargues

Oh, love will make a dog howl in rhyme.
Beaumont & Fletcher

Happiness is a good bank account, a good cook, and a good digestion. *Jean Jacques Rousseau*

When my love swears that she is made of truth,
I do believe her though I know she lies.

Shakespeare

If we take matrimony at its lowest, we regard
it as a sort of friendship recognized by the
police.   *Robert Louis Stevenson*

If a woman wants to hold a man she has only
to appeal to what is worst in him.

Oscar Wilde

A man must be a fool who does not succeed in
making a woman believe that which flatters
her.   *Honore de Balzac*

Love is the business of the idle, but the idle-
ness of the busy.   *Baron Lytton*

Jenny kissed me when we met,
Jumping from the chair she sat in;
Time, you thief, who love to get
Sweets into your list, put that in.

Leigh Hunt

It is a truth universally acknowledged, that a
single man in possession of a good fortune,
must be in want of a wife.   *Jane Austen*

Men, some to business, some to pleasure take;
But every woman is at heart a rake.

Alexander Pope

How a little love and good company improves
a woman. *George Farquhar*

Cleopatra's nose, had it been shorter, the whole
aspect of the world would have been changed.

Blaise Pascal

If you cannot inspire a woman with love of
you, fill her above the brim with love of herself;—all that runs over will be yours.

C. C. Colton

Marriage is the best state for man in general;
and every man is a worse man, in proportion
as he is unfit for the married state.

Samuel Johnson

Love! the surviving gift of Heaven,
The choicest sweet of paradise,
In life's else bitter cup distilled.

Thomas Campbell

Women and maidens must be praised, whether
truly or falsely. *German Proverb*

Married men are horribly tedious when they are good husbands, and abominably conceited when they are not. *Oscar Wilde*

There are two things a real man likes—danger and play; and he likes woman because she is the most dangerous of playthings. *Nietzsche*

Blessed are the forgetful; for they get the better even of their blunders. *Nietzsche*

When Silence speaks for Love she has much to say. *Richard Garnett*

If a man have a lock, which every man's key will open, as well as his own, why should he think to keep it private to himself?

Robert Burton

The conquest of passion gives ten times more happiness than we can reap from the gratification of it.
Sir Richard Steele

Open rebuke is better than secret love.
Old Testament

Nycilla dyes her locks, 'tis said,
But 'tis a foul aspersion.
She buys them black; they therefore need
No subsequent immersion.
Lucilius (tr. Wm. Cowper)

If thou must love me, let it be for nought
Except for love's sake only.
Elizabeth Barrett Browning

If a woman could talk out of the two sides of her mouth at the same time, a great deal would be said on both sides.
George Denison Prentice

How I do hate those words, "an excellent marriage." In them is contained more of wicked worldliness than any other words one ever hears spoken.   *Anthony Trollope*

There is a smile of love,
And there is a smile of deceit,
And there is a smile of smiles
In which these two smiles meet.
                    William Blake

Women, like princes, find few real friends.
                    George Lyttelton

Silence gives consent.   *Oliver Goldsmith*

There are very few people who are not ashamed of having been in love when they no longer love each other.   *La Rochefoucauld*

Love is like linen often changed, the sweeter.
                    Phineas Fletcher

Love: a grave mental disease.   *Plato*

Let men tremble to win the hand of woman, unless they win along with it the utmost passion of her heart.   *Nathaniel Hawthorne*

A continuous dropping on a rainy day and a contentious woman are alike.   *Old Testament*

O lyric Love, half angel and half bird
And all a wonder and a wild desire.
Robert Browning

If men knew how women pass the time when they are alone, they'd never marry.
O. Henry

The moral sense enables one to perceive morality—and avoid it; the immoral sense enables one to perceive immorality—and enjoy it.
Mark Twain

Where my heart lies, let my brain lie also.
Robert Browning

Divorce dates from just about the same time as marriage; I think that marriage is a few weeks older.   *Voltaire*

The more I see of men, the more I like dogs.
Mme. de Stael

I like him and his wife; he is so ladylike, and she's such a perfect gentleman. *Sydney Smith*

Little do women realize that all a man needs under the cerulean dome of heaven is love—and board and clothes.   *Edgar Wilson Nye*

There are people who would never have fallen in love if they had never heard of love.
La Rochefoucauld

Love never dies of starvation but often of indigestion.   *Ninon de Lenclos*

Heaven grant us patience with a man in love!
Rudyard Kipling

When once the young heart of a maiden is stolen, the maiden herself will steal after it soon.
Thomas Moore

Illusion is the first of all pleasures.   *Voltaire*

Venus, a beautiful good-natured lady, was the goddess of love; Juno, a terrible shrew, the goddess of marriage; and they were always mortal enemies.   *Jonathan Swift*

Next to the pleasure of making a new mistress is that of being rid of an old one.
                    William Wycherly

The better part of valor is indiscretion.
                    Samuel Butler

There is a comfort in the strength of love;
'Twill make a thing endurable, which else
Would overset the brain, or break the heart.
                    William Wordsworth

All tragedies are finished by death; all comedies are ended by a marriage.   *Lord Byron*

Money will say more in one moment than the most eloquent lover can in years.

Henry Fielding

Love is like the measles; we can have it but once, and the later in life we have it, the tougher it goes with us.   *Josh Billings*

Men who do not make advances to women are apt to become victims to women who make advances to them.   *Walter Bagehot*

The world's as ugly, ay, as sin,
And almost as delightful.

Frederick Locker-Lampson

If a woman were on her way to her execution, she would demand a little time to put on makeup.   *Sebastien Chamfort*

The magic of first love is our ignorance that it can ever end.   *Benjamin Disraeli*

Kissing don't last; cookery do!

George Meredith

There are worse occupations in this world than feeling a woman's pulse.   *Laurence Sterne*

34

What man wants: all he can get; what woman
wants: all she can't get.

George Denison Prentice

Before I got married I had six theories about
bringing up children; now I have six children,
and no theories.   *Lord Rochester*

To be wise, and love,
Exceeds man's might.   *Shakespeare*

Were it not for imagination, sir, a man would
be as happy in the arms of a chambermaid as
of a duchess.   *Samuel Johnson*

The advantage of the emotions is that they
lead us astray.   *Oscar Wilde*

The tragedy of life is not so much what men
suffer, but rather what they miss.

Thomas Carlyle

To describe happiness is to diminish it.

Stendhal

The first spat in love, as the first misstep in
friendship, is the only one we can turn to good
use.   *Jean de La Bruyere*

It is the wisdom of crocodiles, to shed tears when they would devour.   *Francis Bacon*

An inviolable fidelity, good humour, and complacency of temper, outlive all the charms of a fine face, and make the decays of it invisible.
                                        Sir Richard Steele

A dishonest woman cannot be kept, an honest woman ought not to be kept, necessity is a keeper not to be trusted.   *Robert Burton*

Be plain in dress, and sober in your diet;
In short, my deary, kiss me, and be quiet.
                                        Mary Wortley Montagu

We are never deceived; we deceive ourselves.
                                        Goethe

It is better to play than do nothing.
                                        Confucius

When a man has married a wife he finds out whether her knees and elbows are only glued together.   *William Blake*

Forty years of romance make a woman look like a ruin and forty years of marriage make her look like a public building.   *Oscar Wilde*

A light wife doth make a heavy husband.
                                                    Shakespeare

Some do long for pretty knacks,
And some for strange devices:
God send me that my lady lacks,
I care not what the price is.   *Anonymous*

Beneath this stone my wife doth lie:
Now she's at rest, and so am I!   *Boileau*

Marriage is a very sea of calls and claims, which have but little to do with love.   *Henrik Ibsen*

True love is like seeing ghosts; we all talk about it, but few of us have ever seen one.

La Rochefoucauld

I do not love thee, Doctor Fell.
The reason why I cannot tell;
But this alone I know full well,
I do not love thee, Doctor Fell.

Thomas Brown

Women are won when they begin to threaten.

Old Proverb

Vice is a monster of so frightful mein
As to be hated needs but to be seen;
Yet seen too oft, familiar with her face,
We first endure, then pity, then embrace.

Alexander Pope

Most men employ the first years of their life in making the last miserable.

Jean de La Bruyere

To understand all makes us very indulgent.

Mme. de Stael

His passions make man live, his wisdom merely makes him last. *Sebastien Chamfort*

When our vices leave us, we flatter ourselves
with the credit of having left them.

La Rochefoucauld

Love, like the cold bath, is never negative, it
seldom leaves us where it finds us, if once we
plunge into it, it will either heighten our virtues or inflame our vices.   *C. C. Colton*

They can conquer who believe they can.

John Dryden

He will never worship well the image on the
altar who knew it when it was a trunk of wood
in the garden.   *Spanish Proverb*

The woman one loves always smells good.

Remy de Gourmont

After forty, men have married their habits, and
wives are only an item in the list, and not the
most important.   *George Meredith*

A married philosopher is necessarily comic.

Nietzsche

To love and win is the best thing; to love and
lose, the next best.   *Thackeray*

Many a good hanging prevents a bad marriage.
Shakespeare

Be good and you will be lonesome.
Mark Twain

There is nothing like desire for preventing the things we say from having any resemblance to the things in our minds. *Marcel Proust*

More women grow old nowadays through the faithfulness of their admirers than through anything else. *Oscar Wilde*

The course of true anything never does run smooth. *Samuel Butler*

A sharp tongue is the only edged tool that grows keener with constant use. *Washington Irving*

Conscience is a cur that will let you get past it but that you cannot keep from barking.

Anonymous

Castles in the air cost a vast deal to keep up.

Baron Lytton

Joy to forgive and joy to be forgiven
Hang level in the balances of Love.

Richard Garnett

Perfect love means to love the one through whom one became unhappy.

Soren Kierkegaard

Aversion gives love its death wound, and forgetfulness buries it.   *Jean de La Bruyere*

Love slays what we have been that we may be
what we were not.   *Saint Augustine*

Jealousy is always born with love, but does not
always die with it.   *La Rochefoucauld*

A lover tries to stand in well with the pet dog
of the house.   *Moliere*

Love is an ideal thing, marriage a real thing;
a confusion of the real with the ideal never
goes unpunished.   *Goethe*

The most happy marriage I can picture would
be the union of a deaf man to a blind wife.
          Samuel Coleridge

Tongue; well, that's a very good thing when
it ain't a woman's.   *Charles Dickens*

Love's tongue is in his eyes.
          Phineas Fletcher

Man is born unto trouble, as the sparks fly up-
ward.   *Old Testament*

What female heart can gold despise?
What cat's averse to fish?   *Thomas Gray*

A pretty foot is a great gift of nature.   *Goethe*

Those who dream by day are cognizant of many
things which escape those who dream only by
night.   *Edgar Allan Poe*

The saddest thing that can befall a soul
Is when it loses faith in God and woman.
                                    Alexander Smith

Love is enough, though the world be a-waning.
                                    William Morris

Absence is the enemy of love.
                                    Italian Proverb

Adam was but human—this explains it all. He
did not want the apple for the apple's sake, he
wanted it only because it was forbidden.
                                    Mark Twain

They that are rich in words,
     must needs discover
That they are poor in that which
     makes a lover.   *John Donne*

Keep your eyes open before marriage, and
half-shut afterwards.   *Benjamin Franklin*

Friendship is a disinterested commerce between equals; love, an abject intercourse between tyrants and slaves.

Oliver Goldsmith

He that falls in love with himself will have no rivals. *Benjamin Franklin*

The stage is more beholding to love than the life of man. For as to the stage, love is ever matter of comedies, and now and then of tragedies; but in life it doth much mischief.

Francis Bacon

The measure of a man's real character is what he would do if he knew he would never be found out. *Thomas Macaulay*

The devil can cite Scripture for his purpose.

Shakespeare

She is intolerable, but that is her only fault.

Talleyrand

Love makes all hard hearts gentle.

Old Proverb

As no roads are so rough as those that have just been mended, so no sinners are so intolerant as those that have just turned saints.

C. C. Colton

A good husband is never the first to go to sleep at night or the last to awake in the morning.

Honore de Balzac

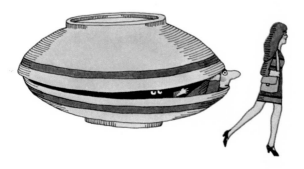

Marriage is a covered dish.   *Swiss Proverb*

We often do good in order that we may do evil
with impunity.   *La Rochefoucauld*

No padlocks, bolts or bars can secure a maiden
so well as her own reserve.   *Cervantes*

Yes—loving is a painful thrill,
And not to love more painful still;
But oh, it is the worst of pain,
To love and not be lov'd again!
                    Anacreon (tr. Thomas Moore)

Those who have free seats at the play hiss first.
                    Chinese Proverb

Courting and wooing
Bring dallying and doing.   *William Camden*

"Home, Sweet Home" must surely have been
written by a bachelor.   *Samuel Butler*

In love, everything is true, everything is false;
it is the one subject on which one cannot ex-
press an absurdity.   *Sebastien Chamfort*

Of all sexual aberrations, perhaps the most pe-
culiar is chastity.   *Remy de Gourmont*

Adam invented love at first sight, one of the greatest labor-saving machines the world ever saw.   *Josh Billings*

Be virtuous and you will be happy; but you will be lonesome sometimes.   *E. W. Nye*

Call no man unhappy until he is married.
          Socrates

I'm glad I'm not a man, for if I were I'd be obliged to marry a woman.   *Mme. de Stael*

Familiarity breeds contempt—and children.
          Mark Twain

Love is like a dizziness,
It winna let a poor body
Gang about his bizziness!   *James Hogg*

Don't be misled into the paths of virtue.
          Oscar Wilde

Love is merely a madness; and, I tell you, deserves a dark house and a whip as madmen do: and the reason why they are not so punished and cured is that the lunacy is so ordinary that the whippers are in love too.   *Shakespeare*

47

A fashionable woman is always in love—with herself.   *La Rochefoucauld*

Men lose more conquests by their own awkwardness than by any virtue in the woman.
                                                            Ninon de Lenclos

No man is an island entire of itself.
                                                            John Donne

If we were not all so excessively interested in ourselves, life would be so uninteresting that none of us would be able to endure it.
                                                            Arthur Schopenhauer

He who cannot love must learn to flatter.
                                                            Goethe

Marriage is neither heaven nor hell; it is merely purgatory.   *Abraham Lincoln*

A thing of beauty is a joy forever. *John Keats*

Men are so made that they can resist sound argument, and yet yield to a glance.
Honore de Balzac

Where none admire, 'tis useless to excel;
Where none are beaux, 'tis vain to be a belle.
George Lyttelton

Had we never lov'd sae kindly,
Had we never lov'd sae blindly,
Never met—or never parted—
We had ne'er been broken-hearted.
Robert Burns

She was one of the early birds,
And I was one of the worms. *T. W. Connor*

Man is lyrical, woman epic, marriage dramatic.
Novalis

To marry a second time represents the triumph of hope over experience.   *Samuel Johnson*

Marriage makes an end of many short follies —being one long stupidity.   *Nietzsche*

All mankind loves a lover.
Ralph Waldo Emerson

If you wish to be loved, show more of your faults than your virtues.   *Baron Lytton*

O sad kissed mouth, how sorrowful it is!
Swinburne

The eternal in woman draws us on.   *Goethe*

The reason lovers are never weary of each other is because they are always talking about themselves.   *La Rochefoucauld*

A woman's whole life is a history of the affections.   *Washington Irving*

Prudery is a form of avarice.   *Stendhal*

When love is concerned, it is easier to renounce a feeling than to give up a habit.

Marcel Proust

We are nearer loving those who hate us than those who love us more than we wish.

La Rochefoucauld

'Tis woman that seduces all mankind, By her we first were taught the wheedling arts.

John Gay

Every woman is infallibly to be gained by every sort of flattery, and every man by one sort or other.   *Earl of Chesterfield*

Gallantry consists in saying empty things in an agreeable manner.   *La Rochefoucauld*

When we are happy we are always good, but when we are good we are not always happy.

Oscar Wilde

The only victory over love is flight. *Napoleon*

A sweetheart is a bottle of wine; a wife is a wine bottle.   *Charles Baudelaire*

The man who can govern a woman can govern a nation. *Honore de Balzac*

That is the nature of women, not to love when we love them, and to love when we love them not. *Cervantes*

Women are like tricks by sleight of hand,
Which, to admire, we should not understand.
William Congreve

A woman cannot guarantee her heart, even though her husband be the greatest and most perfect of men. *George Sand*

A woman can keep one secret—the secret of her age. *Voltaire*

Nothing spoils a romance so much as a sense of humor in the woman.   *Oscar Wilde*

Love works miracles every day: such as weakening the strong, and strengthening the weak; making fools of the wise, and wise men of fools; favoring the passions, destroying reason, and, in a word, turning everything topsy-turvy.
    Marguerite de Valois

'Tis better to have loved and lost than never to have lost at all.   *Samuel Butler*

Those who have loved have little relish for friendship. The devotee of strong drink finds wine insipid.   *Alexander Dumas*

If you are ever in doubt as to whether or not you should kiss a pretty girl, always give her the benefit of the doubt.   *Thomas Carlyle*

The Book of Life begins with a man and a woman in a garden, and it ends with Revelations.   *Oscar Wilde*

A wise man sees as much as he ought, not as much as he can.   *Montaigne*

Nay, 'tis confessed
That fools please women best.   *John Lyly*

Love is too young to know what conscience is;
But who knows not conscience is born of love?
Shakespeare

Some cunning men choose fools for their wives, thinking to manage them, but they always fail.
Samuel Johnson

The man who enters his wife's dressing room is either a philosopher or a fool.
Honore de Balzac

Once made equal to man, woman becomes his superior.   *Socrates*

Men marry because they are tired, women because they are curious; both are disappointed.

Oscar Wilde

Man and wife make one fool. *Ben Jonson*

The whisper of a beautiful woman can be heard farther than the loudest call of duty.

Joseph Joubert

Virtue in women is often merely love of their reputation and of their peace of mind.

La Rochefoucauld

The heart that is soonest awake to the flowers
Is always the first to be touch'd by the thorns.

Thomas Moore

Young men want to be faithful and are not; old men want to be faithless and cannot.

Oscar Wilde

He's a fool that marries; but he's a greater that does not marry a fool. *William Wycherly*

Man begins by making love and ends by loving a woman; woman begins by loving a man and ends by loving love. *Remy de Gourmont*

Even bees . . . know there is richest juice in poison-flowers.   *John Keats*

There is a tide in the affairs of women which, taken at the flood, leads—God knows where.
                                                    Lord Byron

Man was created a little lower than the angels, and has been getting a little lower ever since.
                                                    Josh Billings

There are no little events with the heart. It magnifies everything; it places in the same scales the fall of an empire of fourteen years and the dropping of a woman's glove, and almost always the glove weighs more than the empire.   *Honore de Balzac*

Love that has nothing but beauty to keep it in good health is short-lived.   *Erasmus*

Fools rush in where angels fear to tread.

Alexander Pope

Love as it exists in society is nothing more than the exchange of two fancies and the contact of two epidermises. *Sebastien Chamfort*

A woman is a well-served table, that one sees with different eyes before and after the meal.

Honore de Balzac

Few have borne unconsciously the spell of loveliness. *Whittier*

'Tis strange what a man may do, and a woman yet think him an angel. *Thackeray*

The great question that has never been answered, and which I have not yet been able to answer despite my thirty years of research into the feminine soul, is: What does a woman want? *Sigmund Freud*

Men are men, but Man is a woman.
Chesterton

If a man hears much that a woman says, she is not beautiful. *Haskins*

One can, to an almost laughable degree, infer what a man's wife is like from his opinions about women in general. *John Stuart Mill*

Feminine passion is to masculine as an epic to an epigram. *Kraus*

All the books extolling the simple life are written by men. *Feather*

Most women are not so young as they are painted. *Max Beerbohm*

Women who are either indisputably beautiful or indisputably ugly are best flattered upon the score of their understandings. *Chesterfield*

There is nothing like desire for preventing the things we have to say from having any resemblance to the things in our minds.

Marcel Proust

One half, the finest half, of life is hidden from the man who does not love with passion.

Henri Beyle

The pleasure of love is in loving. We are happier in the passion we feel than in that we inspire.

La Rochefoucauld

What a miserable world! Trouble if we love, and trouble if we do not love.

Count de Maistre

Of all the paths leading to a woman's love, pity is the straightest.

Beaumont and Fletcher

The punishment of those who have loved women too much is to love them always.

Joubert

The life of a woman may be divided into three epochs; in the first she dreams of love, in the second she makes love, in the third she regrets it.

St. Prosper

A husband is a plaster that cures all the ills of girlhood. *Moliere*

Marriage must be a relation either of sympathy or of conquest. *George Eliot*

The reason why so few marriages are happy is because young ladies spend their time in making nets, not in making cages. *Swift*

In buying houses and taking a wife, shut your eyes and commend yourself to God.
Italian Proverb

He knows little who will tell his wife all he knows. *Richard Steele*

For God's sake hold your tongue, and let me love. *John Donne*

Set in Monotype Walbaum, a light, open typeface designed by Justus Erich Walbaum (1768-1839), who was a type founder at Goslar and at Weimar.
Printed on Hallmark Eggshell Book paper.
Designed by Harald Peter.